and everything in-between
Poetry for Reconnecting, Releasing & Reclaiming Parts of Self

Andrea R. Freeman

Copyright © 2024 by Andrea R. Freeman

All rights reserved.

No part of this book may be reproduced in any form or by any electronic or mechanical means, including information storage and retrieval systems, without written permission from the author, except for the use of brief quotations in a book review.

❦ Created with Vellum

To all the poets who recited my thoughts, I hope I can be your voice as well...

Contents

Introduction	ix
Exploring This Book:	xi
Section One: Visions: (Poems for Reconnecting)	1
Oc Md	3
Vision Board	5
Those City Lights	7
Soon...We'll Be Back	9
Time – Out	11
Itchin	13
Temporarily Empty	15
Molting	17
Eye of The Beholder	19
Change of Reason	21
Unchartedly Beautiful	23
That Monday in July	25
The Glitch	27
Whispers in The Sky	29
The Same, But Different	31
West	33
Knights, Princesses & All That Fairy Tale Stuff	35
Treasure Seeker	37
Shadows of the Past	39
The Fate of Stone and Water	41
Transport	43
Home	45
e V e R y B o D y is different...	47
As Above	49
Snow Day	51
Those Narrow Blue Streets	53
Heart Space	55
Section Two: Memories (Poems for Releasing)	57
An Old Tower Remains	59
"Whispers Before Screams"	61

The Glee Club	63
19 thru 22	65
Proved Him Wrong	67
The Philosophical Wild Animal	69
How?	71
Blue	73
Show Me Your Nights	75
Sober	77
I Remember Us	79
Untitled	81
Lighthouse	83
Confessional	85
Wasting Wine	87
Nobody Slow Dances Anymore	89
Water & Earth	91
Yesterday Will Have to Be Enough	93
Rhythmic	95
Let Us Help You	97
Untitled	99
Saylor	101
My Heart, My Heart, My Heart	103
Eternity	105
The Universe	107
Crimson	109
Levitate	111
One Light	113
Afterlife	115
Good Morning	117
Lullaby	119
Beauty Unraveled	121
Equivalencies	123
The Whole Time	125
Paint Dry	127
Untitled	129
Hubby Love Philosophy	131
Anywhere	133
Section Three: And Everything in Between: (Poems for Reclaiming)	137

Extensions	139
Some nights when you can't sleep...	141
Umbrellas	143
We Forgot How to Skip	145
Lines Crossed	147
Lately	149
Tending	151
Knowing the Difference	153
On My Radar	155
L.O.L	157
As I Ground	159
Simple Reminders	161
Keep Peddling	163
Cycles	165
That is all	167
Untitled	169
Can You Use It in a Sentence?	171
Words Neglected, Part 2	173
Daily Lessons from Trees	175
Bouquet	177
Defining Moment	179
Promise to Sunrise	181
About the Author	183
About The Photographer	185

Introduction

You weren't supposed to read this...

About six years ago, my life cried out for attention. I was stifled by patterns and choices that kept circling back to unfulfilling experiences. I was working a job I hated, surrounded by people who told me to *"stay in my lane,"* and was trying to understand parts of my life that yearned for closure. While writing another book at the time, I also started writing poetry on my bus rides into the office, as a way to vent, create & heal. Immersing myself deeper into reading and writing the soul of poetry, I loved the escape and comfort I felt while listening to music & tuning into my poetic voice. It became clearer that the other book I was working on would have to wait its turn. Poetry was my spirit animal.

And so now, within your hands is a book you originally weren't supposed to read, but here, I share stories of reconnecting, releasing and reclaiming parts of myself, that I didn't know were needed. My hope is that you find this journey for yourself as well while reading these pages. My poems are how I've navigated my

Introduction

life so far through people, places, visions, memories and everything in between.

I tell stories, some are my own, some are of others', some are about relationships, life purpose, observations & past life memories. To dig even deeper, you'll find spaces & corners of inspiration, fulfillment, wonderment, frustration, adventure, favorite places, words unsaid, fantasy, confusion, humor, draining jobs, annoyances, gratitude, impatience, unrequited love, closure, exhaustion, being in love, sadness, excitement, revelations and so much more. And throughout all this, I have found some answers along the way, and for those that haven't arrived, I've discovered rather a new sense of balance instead.

What is fulfilling and surprising about writing poetry is how much I love the rawness of telling different lengths of stories, whether it's one sentence per poem or two pages. It tells just enough for as much as you need it to, and it's never really finished. You can shorten your poem, or add three together, and it takes on a whole new vibe that you appreciate down the road.

My favorite moments while writing this book, were the musical backdrops that accompanied me along my nature walks. Some artists I've listened to along my woodland trails, were ones I've connected with before, and others I met along the way. My team included Wildes, Bob Moses, Shaed, Florence and the Machine, Halsey, Taylor Swift, London Grammar, The Revivalists, Daughter, Vera Blue...just to name a few. If you really listen, you'll discover that songs & poems are so interchangeable. These forms of expression are the beat and melody of every particle of your being. Sometimes the songs you listen to, just like reading poetry, carry additional meanings than how they were originally intended to be created.

Exploring This Book:

You'll find that this book is broken down into three sections. Please feel free to read these sections in any order you prefer. There is no *"precise"* way to read these poems. Let your intuition guide you as to where to begin, or restart within this book. Close your eyes and thumb through these pages, stopping at the section you are guided/drawn to read – at any given moment of the day. You can also interpret these poems whichever way you feel is calling to you.

Section One: Visions (Poems for Reconnecting): This section reveals the places that I've visited; whether in a tangible way, or in my mind's eye, favorite destinations, places I tried to get away from or get to, my past life landmarks, places that have guided me, made me stronger and added the missing pieces of who I am.

Section Two: Memories (Poems for Releasing) This section tells the stories of those deep, rooted relationships that have ended, are unfinished, that are whole, that have enriched my life, left me confused, needed to escape to and from, spoke to me in the night, and remained in my heart through past lives lived.

Exploring This Book:

Section Three: And Everything in Between (Poems for Reclaiming) This section exposes all those moments in time that don't need a title, that don't need a specific purpose, those moments that just seem to arrive, that can *"just be,"* that fall in between this world and within all of time and space.

My time with this book has brought illumination, growth, confidence, delight, relief, goosebumps and opportunities into my life. And I know there's still more within me to navigate. Within my poems, I hope that these creative worlds inspire you to write, live and explore your own artistic expressions. And when you revisit your own personal spaces, my prayer is that you do so with grace and compassion, enabling you to safely release your emotions within.

Let these visions, memories and everything in-between pulse life into your own inner compass.

Section One: Visions:
(Poems for Reconnecting)

places visited; tangible & within the mind favorite destinations
places to get away from or get to past life landmarks
places that have guided

Oc Md

car anxiously ready windows willingly down
music pleasantly chill
hand freely coasting through air breezes excite
sun roof open, rays for days just four hours and
we're home

we see the signs
we know we're close
everything already feels different, a weight has lifted sea
    oat-lined homes greet us with every
gently sway

You always look the same to us, and it's that constant
that never bores. You welcome us with that same sweet-
    salt air. We're forever connected to you. Nothing
    matters when
we're here.

We'll abide by your lazy routine any day. We
promise to always visit,
promise us you'll never change.

Vision Board

I can see it – it's ours!
We're alone and it's all ours! Where would you like to go first?
Do you want me to hide & you'll seek?
Never thought I'd get lost in something that's ours. Let's create that map!
There's so many choices & themes to get lost in. It feels different and familiar here.
I like all this space
See...I told you, you'd still have room. I see so much potential here.
I love to escape out back and still feel stress free inside. What a lovely space this will be.
We finally have what was meant for us all along. Welcome Home!

Those City Lights

There's something

*Fleeting Momentary Transitory Evanescent Transient
Fugitive there...igniting those city lights*

Some see endless

*Opportunity Advancement Currency Abandonment Crisis
Poverty...igniting those city lights*

I see AM hours of

*Optimism Confidence Vitality Embraces Discovery
Identity...igniting those city lights*

Others see PM hours of,

*Dress Rehearsals Freedom Glances Restlessness Empty
    Promises Flirtations
Passion...igniting those city lights*

Andrea R. Freeman

What ignites your city lights?

Soon...We'll Be Back

What I miss most is turning to your gaze. Reflective pastels along your face.
Our hands intertwined through ocean mist. Feet beneath grounding sand.
Air sweetened with umbrella drinks. This...this is our place.
We can't be there now,
but if you close your eyes with me, we can steal a few moments away.

Time – Out

I sit on these steps of *St. Patrick's Cathedral*, not to pray, but to escape.

It's always around the same time – my window of opportunity for me to sit, before the portal closes at 2pm. It is here, I pretend I'm on vacation, as this feeling is reflected upon the faces who are soaking in this historic sight behind me. I confidently steal their relaxed, starry-eyed movements of being away from their hometown(s) to enjoy sights so foreign to them.

Look at how they just stroll--not a care in the world, not worrying about the weight of their souvenir bags, the clunkiness of a wide angled lens, or the squint of warm freckled light in their eyes.

Look at their comfortable, trendy summer/fall wardrobes and chic backpacks. Look at them -- just gladly pausing to stop and take in the competing noise around them, while eating sprinkled ice-cream cones, not caring as the sweetness drips down.

This...this same noise and chaos around them, that at times, frustrates my overwhelmed mind, is their preferred track on their getaway playlist. This here, is more than just *"people watching."* This is my time-out, from a 9 to 5, to witness bliss, to feel awe, to feel something, and to remember there's more to me than just being the spectator.

Until then...same place, same time...same faces.

Itchin

My legs are tired of sitting. My behind doesn't trust seats.
　　My neck is angry with me.
My ears hate telephone serenades. My voice is done with
　　formalities. My eyes keep getting smaller.
My pen can only compose scribbles. My belly wants rest.
My mind wants nourishment.

My patience is thinner than a string. My status is
　　redundant.

Temporarily Empty

Constantly fighting myself, I'm here – then, I'm not.
I see the answer – but feel the resistance. I wish I could stay consistent.
Wish I could truly break free! I'm trapped in this tug of war.
There's a film that never washes away, and I don't know how to keep it clean.
Feel so grey and beige and other unfulfilled colors. I'm more than this!
I feel the pull.
I just constantly show up – but don't bring the show.
When can I just walk away – without any obligations – without any questions?! Without anything hanging over?!?
I'm tired of thinking. I'm tired of worrying. Why can't I just leave?!
Feeling suffocated. My smile has no strength to meet my eyes... my friends can sense it too.
Have no time to spend time.
An endless cycle of no replenishment.
I see what could be, but can't let the light in.

Andrea R. Freeman

I have to do the work, I just have to do the work.
I just have to strike that key – let it flow – let it go –let it be - but even that can't wake me.
When will I wake up? I need to wake up!! How will I wake up!?! The answer is creative, and if I could just have that time.
I'll be all right....
I'll be all right....

Molting

I just passed myself on 46th & 5th
on 53rd & 3rd
on *Maiden Lane*

I see myself out there, trenching imprints in the sidewalk.
   This never ending dance of,*"What am I doing with my
   life?"* was performed weekdays in front of those
   establishments.

Not the right fit. Predictable.
Stifling.

Same theme, same responsibilities, same attitudes, just
   different buildings to enter, names and faces to
   remember.

I see myself standing there, so frustrated,
so lost,
so drained.

It's like I kept repeating the same dance sequence in

hopes I'd remember the cues for my next move. Still, I had trouble realizing I had to remove those layers that caused me to stumble. But from across the way, my past sees me now, the positive contrast of all this. I've come so far since my dancing days. There's a few more moves in me to learn in this rat race. I'll be making it to the big stage soon. I've started to shed that old skin. I can freestyle now, bet ya didn't know that!

I reassure my past self - with a hopeful nod and a glisten in my eye, that there's just one more move yet to master, and you're free....we'll all be free....

Eye of The Beholder

I love days like these, when you have to go out, and you don't mind being wrapped around a chunky gray-blanketed sky. I don't see it as ominous, or a day to hide with *Netflix*. It invites me to go out and explore and keep my promise to be a tourist for a day in *Midtown*. And there's that right mixture of cool breezes and warmth that allows you to tie your jacket around your waist. I feel like I can get so much done today! I feel like the innocent blah above me, only reflects the patchwork of opportunities left to embrace for today. I'm optimistic, what can I say, as I stare up at a beautiful cloudy day.

Change of Reason

I'm not a fan of repetitive loud noises, expected hustle, and waking up before the birds, but I do love Autumn in NY. The crispness of the air softens my disdain for the 24/7 rush of the city. There's just something about the sunlit glow, crowning a small nature patch in *Bryant Park*, at 8:49am, easing your grudges. It seems to be the only time you won't mind getting up early to travel into *Manhattan* and witness this brief window of this fable.

New York hasn't completely decided if it wants to fully be Fall, but it won't let you suffer that August heat. I can actually feel myself pause on this determined bus and connect with myself for once, and not be annoyed by my crowding neighbor. "*I want to be outside more...not just in Summer,*" I proclaim quietly to myself. I guess it's just something about Autumn in NY. You're promised that so much good, can still come to you. Proof is in the wide strides of those carrying their labeled lattes.

Andrea R. Freeman

Fresh starts, restarts, born again, born anew...each of us a different purpose as the tri-colored leaves has theirs. How refreshing--how surprising, that a city that rushes you to move, can force you to stop and change....change *your* reason....

Unchartedly Beautiful

I stare off into the same sparkling distance, from when I really
didn't know where my life was going. I knew then, that it couldn't keep going the way it was. I watched the hopeful sunrise that day, and prayed that its warm pastels would beam a path--an answer to a more purposeful course.

I stare back now, a year later from this fluid-lined course, smile at my warm-inviting friend, and humbly review all the unknown calls I answered, the times fluctuating in-between, and the healthy risks that improved my life.

As I revisit my solar gaze, there's an unexpected feeling... this new unknown...of not knowing what to do now. At this point I've accomplished almost everything *"I needed to"* – to get to this
tranquil path. I've never lived in this space before. I've always been searching and searching for more answers, and more answers outside myself.

Andrea R. Freeman

But now....now, I'm here--I'm where I need to be--right now with myself...and it feels sooo unchartedly beautiful!! And for the first time, I needn't worry my next move.

That Monday in July

I can't believe I'm sitting here in this blissful silence.
I can't believe I get to witness what others miss
on a day like today...bees having lunch with dandelions,
    the strongest trees fluttering their hellos, gentle
    breezes caressing blades of green, brush stroked cirrus
    clouds, in no rush at all. I'm so grateful I finally
    listened to my intuition and said, "*Fuck it*! *This day is
    mine and I deserve it!*" And I still got so much done out
    here--the most productive four hours spent; with the
    back deck for my desk and the sun as my lamp light; a
    fluorescent cubed room could not compare.

The Glitch

It's the 4th day of October & it seems Mother Nature is restless with her own progress as she tries to catch up for lost time – hurriedly shaking the leaves off barely foliage trees. Perhaps she too has procrastinated on much needed change. The vigorous cold was such a stark contrast to her slip-up two days ago when she allowed us to wear open toe shoes, dresses and shorts. As I sit by my turquoise draped window, I'm grateful for such beautiful, confused chaos…for where in the world can you get two of your favorite seasons in one week? But, isn't that so much like us?

Shadows and light…orchestrated so delicately.

Whispers in The Sky

Is it the earth from afar? Is it the ocean reflected?
Or is it just a snapshot of sky above me?

Feathery, white clouds spoke to me today like Bob Ross
whispering, *"There"*

Is it just *there* like this picture – painted day?
I think I'm just *there* -- somewhere between being in the
moment meets everything else can wait.

The Same, But Different

Sirens on a mission in the distance.
Ice cream truck singing a contrasting, laid-back tune.
    Lawns getting manicured.
Train horn alerting an upcoming destination.

WAIT—this isn't right? WHERE AM I?!

I open my eyes and realize, these are sounds of a place
    once familiar and yet out of place—all competing for
    my attention -- but in my new state of mind, I
    embrace a little bit of home and a little bit of now.

West

    Front porch--strained wood Sunset patterned—chair
      rocking Apron made—frayed threads Face lined
      —Squinting

(Waiting)

    Dedicated hands Worried soul Hard eyes
    Heart of defense

(Promising)

    Dog pacing Gentle breeze
    Chills on sleeved arms Children playing

(Being)

    Time to prepare Fire dancing
    Cast iron yielding Table laden

Andrea R. Freeman

(Living)

    Chair empty Lanterns bowing Shutters sleeping Light
       galloping

(Hopeful)

    Dedicated hands Thankful soul Soft eyes
    Heart of rest

    (Breathing)

Knights, Princesses & All That Fairy Tale Stuff

She's a dreamer
She sees enchanting tales through moving yellow-orange
    trees, along 440.
Why can't it be mystical? Why can't it be a fairytale?

Knights, Castles, Roses, A Dance, A Look, A Time Long Lost

Tall--lavender, beige sway - switches her memories
to and fro. All but to extend her hand, and she would
    instantly know.

Do others see what she feels? Do others feel what she
    sees?

Knights, Castles, Roses, A Dance, A Look, A Time Long Lost
But it is a time long lost, and every day at 7:37am, the
    realm of possibility opens... just enough for her
    enchanted heart to still believe and get carried away
    on her four-wheeled steed....

Knights, Princesses and all that Fairy Tale Stuff

Treasure Seeker

A vessel sails, its course unknown.
Midst the tallest trees, beneath the lowest heavens, it
    ceases to wait.
Its faith lay in the clutches of a hallow purpose.

A persistent chill, blankets her steps back to a path long
    forgotten to him.
Once, warm light, breathed life into these tall trees.
    Unfamiliar now, a swift foreshadowing covers these
    towers.

The heart of the traveler rests his gallant anchor in the
    West, where his material love resides. And where the
    Eastern shores call, a dull shadow rises over his first
    heart of the ocean.

Though his mind, as open and fearless as the blowing
    sails, still can't withstand the spinning greed of his
    compass. No treasure among these four corners can
    save his soul.

Andrea R. Freeman

His purest love smells of sweet salty waves--tastes of exotic fruits. His new found conquest, encrusted with emeralds and crimson gold fare.

Shadows of the Past

There is a log cabin midst the weary, overgrown forest.
Its only inhabitants these days, are misty shadows of memory. The old stone path is laden with dried, confetti leaves.
At the hour of two in the morn',
a dance of gold flashes through the cabin's empty spaces.

Those who had lived, who died, return for a constant search of rest.
Clues are smudged within mud patches, tangled around old, stretched branches, twirling high toward the scented, damp air.

Yet, there is no one willing, nor brave enough to admit.
The cabin breathes for the soul who will free it from its captives. Who will take a stand for those who now roam in silence?
Earthly cares, broken promises, shattered webs, all ended in one fired shot. Scattered is the youth of the forest. Nothing breathes nor wakes. All is gray, cold and twisted except for a sliver of golden hope to be freed.

The Fate of Stone and Water

Do you want to feel your past?
Not a desired path for some, but there is a place that
    offers. Once before laid out, now must be quested.

Go to the forest's edge, exhale the secret word toward the
    sky, and take a leap of faith. There you will find a
    circular stone passage, with clear, liquid fill. A quick
    dampness in the air greets you. The soaked and weary
    branches are your signposts. Low fog surrounds your
    dwelling, a transparent cushion for what awaits.

The Well patiently welcomes you in its hidden space.
    What will you ask of it? Are you ready for its reply?
You anxiously grip the cracked, stoned sides. Fear not the
    sound of broken twigs, for it is the guardian of the
    Well, who longed for your return.

Rain begins to roll down your impatient face, spilling
    with fright into the all-seeing element. A rush of
    bitter, sharp--pierces your regretful hands. The water
    awakens, its dark rippled shadows reveal your truth.

Andrea R. Freeman

Drink it in

Transport

Rain carefully fell amongst the demanding city, with the
    gentlest touch of warmth,
reminiscent of undisturbed woods. And in that moment,
    on my break,
if I didn't have to go back to those torrential fluorescents,
    I would have leaned-in, unshielded.

Home

can't decide if it was the flickering leaves of a sweet,
    Summer's night,
the sea oats swaying along the shore, bamboo whistling in
    the gardens,
or the three words you whispered, that carried me home.

e V e R y B o D y is different...

oCeAnS encourage....don't play small LaKeS
    speak....listen to your heart
RiVeRs bend....take more risks
cReEkS cleanse....clear your mind PoNds play....trust your
    inner child

As Above

On a mid-Winter's walk, a single leaf above,
twirls on the thinnest branch, with the slightest of ease.
Many storms have barreled before, and yet, this single
   leaf still holds.

As I pause and admire this impressive strength, is it so, or
   does stubbornness reside here?
Why do we hold on?
Is it to prove something?
Do we just have the will to do so? Or is the changing of
   inner cycles just as challenging?

Snow Day

I didn't realize how much I was hurting, until an Angel in the snow comforted me.

I didn't realize how much my inner child
needed this day, until I saw my face in that photograph
.

I didn't realize how to let go, until it was time to trust-
fall.

Those Narrow Blue Streets

#TommyRivsPoetry (*poetry prompt title created by author/poet Alicia Cook*)

    That's what it feels like, complete tunnel vision.

    You forget the list of friends to call. You forget how to read affirmations.
    You forget you've been down this narrow road before.

    But then, it somehow clicks! You just GET UP!
    You put your sneakers on and you run! Playlist at the ready.

    The road ahead may still feel narrow, but somehow, your blue heart starts to love again.

Heart Space

and as I leaned in,
I placed my hand over his heart, looked into his eyes
and said,
this....this here, is my home.

Section Two: Memories (Poems for Releasing)

relationships that have ended-- are unfinished--
that are whole- escaped to and from, unrequited love, loved-
ones,

self-love, spoke to in the night, remained in the heart,
past lives

An Old Tower Remains

(Circa 2003 – the poem that started it all)

    An old tower remains.
    Its crooked stone bends in sorrow. Lifeless in a chair,
    she only feels the movement of her waking eyes.

    Thick veils of spun white, blocks thin natural light.
    Her tears turn to dust as these disperse around her dried,
        cracked face.

    With her cackling grin, she reviews her immoral deeds.
    Dark corners of deceit, intent and fear have delivered her
        to the final resting place...eternal waiting.
    She grasps the touch of familiar seedlings, but her
        extensions fall through like rising fog
    over rolling mountains. Threads of tangled webs lay
        interlocked all around her.

    Like the chains of those forged in life, her tattered,
        quilted blanket holds no warmth nor security.
    This is cold woven, the fabric of her being.

"Whispers Before Screams"

#TommyRivsPoetry (*poetry title prompt created by author/poet Alicia Cook*)

>Everyone has antennas,
>their own intuition receivers. Mine is during dream-state.
>
>It wasn't enough to avoid those triggered moments with
>   you. It wasn't enough to bide my freedom of speech.
>Something always taunted an explosion with you.
>
>But within the night,
>my receiver turned into "The Scream" of 1893 Mouth W I
>   D E -- FULL of forced, whispers that jolted me
>   awake!
>
>I knew in three days we would fight. That was my only
>   warning.

The Glee Club

Hello Boredom, my stubborn friend. Hello Frustration, my reliable confidant.
Hello Moodiness, my unpredictable acquaintance. Hello Stress, my nagging companion.
Hello Impatience, my feisty comrade. Hello Exhaustion, my draining colleague. Hello Unmotivated, my prompt associate. Hello Bitchiness, my masked contact.
Hello Grey, my washed-out chum. Hello Worry, my tense pal.
Hello Doubt, my forgetful buddy.
Hello Overwhelment, my greedy supporter. Hello Procrastination, my envious collaborator. Hello Unqualified, my cunning attendant.
Hello Sensitive, my intuitive ally.

19 thru 22

He believed photographs were for those who couldn't
  remember. He freely gave red & white twist ties as
  promise rings.
He stole hearts with the sway of his mischievous floor-
  length coat.

Nineteen, new girl in school.
Deciding to choose between him & another:
Casual / Cool & Tall – soft white t-shirt, jeans light-blue,
  or the mischievous one above.

Dave Matthews Band always played. Perfect gentleman –
  courted conversations, under the stars of an impatient
  night.

He noticed a shy girl in a class where they learned to
  speak up. He was an unlikely choice, but proved his
  time was valuable. They laughed over her newfound
  skill of holding chopsticks.

Golden hair, cobalt eyes,

Andrea R. Freeman

every visit, a bouquet of surprise.
Oh, but did those sunflowers mesmerize!

Music class, hat backwards, his tempted lean-back sprawl.
    He surprised her with his attraction, confessional.
She admired him more for his respect of her limits.

Biology class, not her strong suit, but his wit was his.
    They were enticed by what they weren't ready for.
Neither realized they were already each others'.

Crushes, unexpected allure, uncharted uniqueness, naïve
    potential, lessons passed...the college years.

Proved Him Wrong

She feels in his eyes, disappointment glaring.
She didn't *"let herself go,"* or have the allure of desperation
    reflecting in her eyes.
Guess the *"you'll never find anyone like me,"*
wears well on her after all.

The Philosophical Wild Animal

Ever wonder if the person you dream about – ever dreams about you?

Do you wonder if that person felt that you dreamt about him/her the next day?

Is it possible you both dreamed about each other in the same night?

They say if you dream about someone, they're thinking about you. They also say if you dream about that person,
it reflects aspects of yourself. Interpretation is in the eye of the dreamer.
I was shocked to see him with my eyes closed, but not shocked to wake wanting to meet once more. As dreams teach and dreamers learn, I discovered he is the archer, guiding me to higher passions. He's that one fire you don't mind feeling the flames.

Andrea R. Freeman

I wonder what he learned that night. I wonder if he needed to see me too.

How?

HOW does one look raise the heat?
HOW does one look vanish all surroundings? HOW does
    one look remember without admitting? HOW does
    one look change who I am?
HOW does one look make no promises?
HOW does one look hold all the answers with unresolved
    doubt? HOW does one look...so handsomely,
    carelessly --
act so selfishly-cool?

how could I let one look – masquerade it all?

Blue

There's a sweetness there, but when I look closer,
your iris-blues show the side I want more.

Why does time arrive late,
and taunt us with what we can't have?

We only have just a short while – enough time to check-in
    and catch-up. Perhaps that was part of the blueprint.

We've only scratched the surface...

Show Me Your Nights

Show me how you move-- From day to night,
your flow intrigues my skin.

Always a party! Always the high-life! A world unknown,
I want in!

I know it's temporary.
It's just those city lights, reflecting this dream.
You make it so real though.

Your night you can pay.
Your night washes it all away. Your night I can stray.
Your night shines my day.

Show me your nights. I want in.

Sober

He's that one more drink too many – my favorite,
dreadful hangover. And I'll lie and say I'm balanced
 enough to walk a straighter path, but my heart will
 stumble.
My mind will take the keys from my soul, and drive me
 crazy for another sober day.

The first pour though is always the most freeing, so
 innocent and full of endless possibilities. The third,
 gets you so much closer to what you know you can
 never have. If you're willing to have a fourth or fifth,
 then you my dear,
are either brave, hopeful, or simply the fool.

But I'm recovering, cleaning up this dependency that
 these past lives try and mix-up. We're only here to
 check in as friends...this time, and I'll have to drink to
 that at least!

I Remember Us

In my dreams you're there.
In my dreams we are there again – but it's not a dream.
    Innocent memories of all that was--what could be,
and will never be--all my senses reveal unattainable
    authenticities.

I want to tell you
I want to show you
I want you to remember
I want you to feel us I want you to tell me
I want you to show me
I want it to be now I want it to be real

The heavy pull within, reveals my centered truth.
    Reminds me why
Reminds me of the hurt Reminds me of chances lost

Do you remember? Do you recognize? Do you feel it too?

I want to tell you
I want to show you

Andrea R. Freeman

I want you to remember
I want you to feel us I want you to tell me
I want you to show me
I want it to be now I want it to be real

It only gets stronger, but ever so restrained.
Yet I should leave the past – a life once lived, behind.

Maybe one life we'll get it right.

Maybe you'll learn then. Maybe I'll learn now.

Do you remember? Do you feel it too?

Lighthouse

I still look for you in songs written
to validate memories I'm not sure existed.

Discrediting myself in false hopes that it was me
you still listened.

I lay my head, not to dream,
but to see your forehead against mine within the ether.

I reach out through this enchanted room to validate
    once more
what I can't quite prove.
This mirage of hope is blinding.
It's exhausting how I can't keep my word not to care.

Are you finally awake from hibernation, as I prepare for
    mine?
And yet you tangle these heart strings, as you leave me
    behind.

Andrea R. Freeman

Ignoring us was never the answer,
and I'm not sure you'll ever find us again, but I'll be here,
    playing these songs -- like a lighthouse guides the
    shore.

Confessional

And so it was done... in blue and white,
folded—sealed—delivered.

She had to.
She had to know... no matter the answer!

It was the only way she could understand; the only way to
    truly embrace this reality. She wasn't afraid, and that
    was frightening. Her confidence was her only reliance.
Yet within this poise, she could fall.

Could it all just fall?
Could it all be more complicated? Could it be worse than
    she thought? But she had to know, to no longer feel
    and see alone.

There is no bliss with ignorance; there's only a hope
There is no rapture in release; there's only a realization.

And so it was...
Received – unsealed – unfolded, read and aware.

Andrea R. Freeman

She looks up, her heart leaps from her empty waiting room. The confession is his hands. Her answer is in real time.

Wasting Wine

Every sip, memories are quenched.
Every taste, imagination spills endlessly.

And as you pour another glass, you're hoping we'll
    disappear into another hazy story
of what was.

Nobody Slow Dances Anymore

It's not our song, but if we admitted everything, it would
    be. As we make circles on the floor,
our heart beats this track.
We look into each other's eyes knowing we had a good
    run, but we never moved off the ground.
My head on your shoulder, replays all I imagined it would
    be. Your hands around me, cradles what escaped.
We slowly extend our arms,
finding our hands like friends promising… "If you ever
    need anything. I'm here."
In the silence of a slow dance, it's haunting never to sing.

Water & Earth

I can't blame you for your careless, free-spirit.
I can't blame you for your charming, restlessness.

I can't blame you for the ebb and flow of your impatient soul, always meandering – sometimes finding shore, but never lingering long enough to ground.

I can't blame you for wanting to explore what's around the bend, amongst uncharted waters. For where I am fixed and solid, you must go fluidly. I know you're trying to find us out there, but that was a long time ago.

I can't blame myself -- expecting the same fervent wave to kiss twice. You know I never liked change.

If ever there was that one thread tethering us both, let it be one that tried to tame your elements.

Yesterday Will Have to Be Enough

You're preoccupied today. I'm not in your view,
it's only fair.
What could we really do with yesterday? But it aches.
And maybe it's because I only see what I want us to be
 And you won't stay around for what you can't have us
 be. Time keeps getting in the way.
Our choices are building the distance. Maybe it's
 protection?
What did you do that I pushed you away? What did I do
 that made you stray?
Too many pieces are setting us apart.
But when I'm in your view, I come alive, and in that
 moment, yesterday is enough.

Rhythmic

I'm not grudging on you.
This isn't a typical breakup...
there are just some songs I'm not ready to let go of yet.

I'm not pinning over borrowed CD's...
it's just these tracks tell how we met, when I fell in, and
    got lost, why I returned, and what made me finally
    leave.

I'm not holding on...I just need to remember, so I don't
    buy the same record again.

Let Us Help You

I know....
I know you're done.
I know you're giving up.
I know you can't see why.
I know you don't want to feel.

Please know I need you. We all need you here.
Please know you do have a purpose. Please know we can
    help you here.

You are the world, and the world lives within you. You
    and I are here for a reason.
Please know you can get through this.

We'll find your strengths. We'll find your happiness. We'll
    find your justice.
We'll find your laughter. We'll find your spark.
We'll find YOU!

Give your life a chance!

Andrea R. Freeman

Please know I need you. We all need you here.
Please know you do have a purpose. Please know we can
    help you here.

See your light through the dark.
This too shall pass, like rolling summer storms.

I'm right here through words I'm right here through hugs
I'm right here through smiles
I'm right here through messages I'm right here through
    prayers
I'm right here through tears
I'm right here through laughter I'm right here through
    listening
We all need you here!
Please know you do have a purpose. Please know we can
    help you here.

While I slept, You cradled.
While I stressed, You listened.
While I complained, You waited.
While I doubted, You showed.
While I feared, You spoke.
While I procrastinated, You nudged.
While I yelled, You understood.
While I cried, You grounded.
While I stumbled, You encouraged.
While I dreamed, You celebrated.
While I loved, You rejoiced.
While I danced, You sang.
While I transformed, You admired.
While I laughed, You glowed.
While I prayed, You answered.

Saylor

Have some time before my birthday dinner with friends.
    39 this year...geez, where did the time go?
I love this room, it's the only one with a side balcony.
    Leaning back in one chair, the other holds my sandy
    toes. Have a pen & notebook in my lap, in case I get
    inspired.

Seagulls sing overhead, wishing me well.
Light breezes hug my exposed - slightly, tanned shoulders.
    Wind chimes & children's laughter are in perfect
    harmony. Bicycles respond with patterned, rhythm
    over the flip-flopped boardwalk. Ocean waves add
    that thunderous back beat.

Birthday calls are off the hook. I'm just listening &
    observing collectively on this salty, sweet *Beach Walk*
    vacation.

Staring up at those pillow cumulus's, a saxophone plays...I
    close my eyes...*Careless Whisper, Star Wars* theme *and*

Andrea R. Freeman

Happy Birthday...entertainment before dinner...how lucky am I?!

Thank you Saylor, you so made my day! See you at dinner!

My Heart, My Heart, My Heart

How do you miss someone you never met?
How do you feel his heart's rhythm and not have danced?
How do you trust his words without the touch of his
 hand? How do you know he's near with just the rise of
 your breath?
How do you know the future
when looking into the eyes of your past?

Eternity

I knew it was you
when my heart plunged.
I knew it was you
when my chest fluttered.
I knew it was you
when my breath skipped.

I knew it was you
when your eyes liked mine.
I knew it was you
when your voice missed mine.
I knew it was you
when your words kissed mine.
I knew it was you
when our past intertwined.

The Universe

It was along her contours,
he found his way back home.
And he would trace the stars over & over until the
　　right path
lead him back to her.

Crimson

Depending on your view, the spark is setting,
as we streak across the horizon.
I finally see your shadows where once, you only showed
 crimson.
Don't mistaken this heat for longevity

.

Levitate

It's just me. Now.
Here....in this deafening silence.
There's no spark. Something was taken. Something was ripped away.
I'm floating in a lower space.
Very different from last you saw me.
It was innocent then. It was soulful then. Now...it's just excruciatingly real.
Why surface to only be submerged again? I'm tired. I don't want to play anymore.
Time to detach from this timeline and levitate toward solid ground.

One Light

I don't know why I keep looking for you. With every
   sound, every movement,
I think your arrival is near.
It's like you never left and yet, it's been ages.
Our hearts are synchronized and yet haven't beat for a
   thousand years.
I have no real memory of us and yet, it's all I can
   remember.
So, I will continue to leave one light on, until one day, you
   find us.

Afterlife

Maybe that's where we'll meet... somewhere between lessons learned and new mistakes made.

Maybe that's where we'll find each other, somewhere between this life and the next.

But I don't want to rush this.
It's just a role we have to play. We'll get it right someday.
Our souls will always remember our eternity.

Good Morning

My favorite sound?

Hearing him fiddle in the kitchen,
as I awake within these cradling sheets.

Lullaby

Sometimes, it's not the blanket on the bed that comforts
    and keeps me warm.
It's the lightest rain tapping on my window. The moonlit
    glow of another phase.
The rustic sunrise gleaming through.
The sound of your breath as you dream a lil more.

These threaded fabrics tuck it all in, Keeps it all safe,
Keeps it evermore.

Beauty Unraveled

You say my beauty does not reside along my curves, nor
 run through my hair,
or color my cheeks.

You say my beauty is how...

my hair sticks-up in the morning, as my groggy eyes say
 hello.
when I sob out-loud trying to figure out my life.
how passionate I am doing what's right, even if I'm the
 only one. when I curl up, blanket under neck,
 watching my favorite show. how I wear oversized
 sweatshirts with a messy bun to write.
You remind me that the beauty you see, resides in my
 Honesty
Love Patience Laughter Silliness
Communication Passion
Uniqueness Creativity Harmony Confidence

You further encourage that my beauty can still be found

amongst the unmotivated, lost and moody days, for you know it's only me trying to do better.

Thank you for seeing all my beautiful sides, even when I couldn't feel it from within.

Equivalencies

Sometimes......

A day can feel like a week
A week can feel like a month A month can feel like a year
A year can feel like a lifetime ago
A lifetime ago can feel like an eternity

Somehow.......

You make all this feel...like no time at all.

The Whole Time

An old friend surprised me today. I can't believe how long it's been since last we communicated. *Her hands* still looked *youthful*. *Her demeanor,* still so *hopeful & sincere*. In the brief moment we shared, I finally understood what it felt to truly *love her--* to *appreciate* how far she's come, all that she's *accomplished*, even if she didn't think she advanced at all. It was *so powerful...* I had to close my eyes and *cradle my heart*.

Through all her trials and errors, she didn't lose *her sweetness*, not once! I *admire her* will to do better and find ways to break pesky old habits, even if she still felt guilty for not trying hard enough.

I think what struck me most about her visit, were her hands. There was so *much innocence, gentleness, experience, wisdom, and strength* there. She's truly lived so many *transformations,*
including the one she's currently in, and it was so *humbling* to recognize the one version in particular, that never left her side.

I'm *grateful* for that version, for *my being* wouldn't exist without her childlike innocence, that strength to keep fighting for a better day-- a more *fulfilling life*, while still *remembering to smile*.

Don't be fooled by that version of *her naivety*...there's so much *confidence, uniqueness, creativity* and *grace* there. *She's no fool*. There's so much more for her yet to explore, *so much more potential* waiting to be embraced. Everyone sees it...now it's time for her to *see it within herself*.

I'd so love to introduce you to her. Though, you might have met her once before. Perhaps you too have a friend like this? Have you been in touch lately? When's the next time you can meet? *"If you have to ask, you'll never know. If you know, you need only ask." (line from The Deathly Hallows by J.K. Rowling)*

Paint Dry

I love my life with you! - I say to myself as I sit across this checkered, pizzeria dinner table, looking at your squishy, cute face. There's no games, no drama, no doubts. I can truly be myself, and comfortably live in my own skin.

We've got that *"I can watch paint dry with you,"* kinda love.

Do you have any idea the world you have given us? Just when I thought my life wouldn't go far, and all the bullshit I've been through, I met you again, and we traveled *(and not always out of the country)*.

Sitting here chatting with you,
my mind starts to wonder further.....

Is it possible to love you more this very second, than the last, and then more the next? To miss you every day, even while you sleep? Is it possible your freckled, hazel eyes can embrace my soul? That you can be sweet, handsome, sexy, classy, hysterical, adorable, energetic, calming and adoring all in one?

Andrea R. Freeman

Is it possible to cuddle with your cuteness and still be ignited by your love?
To not having all the answers, and still feel secure with someone? Is it possible to be this supported, even when others didn't have the courage to do the same? To have your hand on my cheek,
heal all my aches?

Is it possible your jokes make my dimples hurt every time? To say "I Love You" without the "Too"
Is it possible to live in a small space, and not fight? That your shoulder to lay upon still feels just right?

Is it possible to talk about life in Starbucks and not feel weird? To still have date nights and enjoy low-key places?
Is it possible to love it when you nap or play video games while I write this book?
To still respect each other even if we agree to disagree?
Is it possible to feel sad if the other doesn't go grocery shopping with the other?

To still have patience when family life gets challenging?
Is it possible to still love me even if I'm "hangry" or moody from lack of sleep, or frustrated with life? To be silent without the need of a word?

I hope & pray it's still possible for others to live this *"pinch me"* love, as you my love have shown me every promising day, that it is.

Hubby Love Philosophy

*"I'm not worried." "Don't overthink!" "We'll figure it out."
"We've got plenty of time."
"We've got more than enough." "Let them say something, you know the truth!" "You got this Lovey Face!"*

Anywhere

If I could do it all again,
I would, under the highest, cathedral trees.
Our witnesses would be the delicate sway of adventurous
    vines, stubborn wildflowers
and shy, woodland dwellers.

If I could do it all again,
I would, near the salty break and sweet ebb of the
    shoreline. Our witnesses would be the ruby sunset,
cool sand beneath our toes, and curious seagulls.

If I could do it all again,
I would, within an ancient castle of our ancestors.
Our witnesses would be, gilded portraits, ornate
    tapestries, and melodious bagpipes.

If I could do it all again,
I would, over the lushest, rolling green hills.
Our witnesses would be gallant horses, cleansing rain, and
    our home made of unyielding logs.

Andrea R. Freeman

If I could do it all again,
I would... anywhere, any lifetime, with you.

Section Three: And Everything in Between: (Poems for Reclaiming)

> moments that don't need a title,
> moments that arrive,
> moments that can *"just be,"*
> observed moments that fall in-between this world,
> and within all of time and space.

Extensions

(first published in the Pennsylvania Bards 2023 Anthology Book)

>They stand tall amongst the harshest elements.
>>Sometimes twisting and bending, not in defeat, rather in limitless space and time.
>
>And if they fall, it is not without a fight.
>Some see them weep, some hear them laugh, some feel their wrath,
>but they are all just beauty.
>
>Their true power isn't just from their thickened positions or thinnest stances,
>rather from their inner-lined growth, exposing their true wisdom.
>
>They are focused, adaptable, true survivors, in their detailed transformations.
>
>They can be dark and bare, and still sleep peacefully.
>>They can awake with the slightest flicker of texture.
>>They can smell of the sweetest, shimmering green.

Extensions

They can radiate with the deepest, ripple of crimson and
    gold, And be brave enough to slumber once more.
They're admired from their yielding reach, to their
    delicate stretch. Cascading purity, breath, and eternal
    love over all who dwell.
They provide balance where there is chaos, value where
    there is lack,
and shelter where there is vulnerability.

You can stand in its shade, cast your eyes above,
and see the gentle sway of your questions answered.

Oh, how they endlessly teach us all, no matter our skin.
Just look up, sit with them, feel their past,
and learn from within.

Some nights when you can't sleep...

> I think it's because you have words left unsaid, that
>   someone is thinking about you,
> that your anxieties aren't done with you yet, that you
>   have much more to grow into,
> that the moonlight is still whispering in your ear, that
>   your ego still bullies you no matter your age, that your
>   crystals need cleansing,
> that there's a song that still needs a melody, that there's a
>   poem that still needs a lyric, there's a book that still
>   needs a hero,
> that there's an angel that still needs saving, that your
>   bladder calls too much,
> that there's a constant drip of things to do, that you still
>   hurt from their words,
> that there's a mother who still thrives for her kids, that I
>   can't wait to hear what you'll say next,
> that I will miss you while I sleep, and so...I will watch you
>   dream.

Umbrellas

Some are invasive Some are hesitant Some are massive
   Some are slight

Hiding//Shielding/Like You and Me

Some are obnoxious Some are delicate Some are tricky
   Some are fluid

Hiding/Shielding/Like You and Me
Some are clever Some are stubborn
Some are discourteous Some are supportive

Hiding/Shielding/Like You and Me

Some are borrowed Some are new Some are lost Some are
   collected

Hiding/Shielding/Like You and Me

We Forgot How to Skip

It seems we have forgotten how to smile, say yes with confidence, trust who holds our hand. We forgot how not to worry about the future, how to splash in a puddle, how to wear the brightest colors on the rainiest of days. We forgot how to love harmoniously with both mind and heart, and how to be grateful for the tiniest of blessings. We forgot how to silence the noise and just skip to the rhythm of our soul. A fair-haired—young girl dressed all in pink, skipping in-hand with her father toward the relentless--demanding city, reminds me of what we've all forgotten, but had always the power to embrace.

Lines Crossed

As children, they told us to color within the lines, and we rebelled with loops, circles and zig zags.

As adults they tell us to go within, and we rebel with light up screens, distractions and other's opinions.

Lately

Been holding on to a lot lately. Been not knowing a lot lately. Been questioning a lot lately. Been holding my breath lately.

But on the *exhale*
not having all the answers,
means I'm getting a lot better lately.

Tending

I tend to procrastinate when I'm overwhelmed. I tend to
 overthink when I'm overwhelmed.
I tend to doubt when I'm overwhelmed.
I tend to shut down when I'm overwhelmed.

But this time, I will tend to what matters & d e t a c h
 from all the rest.

Knowing the Difference

It's not that I don't know.
It's just that, I'm not ready.
...and that's ok.

On My Radar

There's something about a looming hurricane that makes an August sky feel, like Winter is a day away. Ruffled creases of dark blue and grey, makes you want to stay away.

Change is coming.

It was the most stagnant, quiet you ever witnessed amongst the trees and through the grass, but if you listened closer, you might feel the roots gripping on tighter, bracing the shift.

Change is near.

The calendar might say August 4th, but my internal clock still ticks March 2020. We're only eight months old, but eternity weighs unknowingly heavy. We expected so much from this year and now it's demanding so much from us.

On My Radar

It's crazy how Mother Nature must bring us together by
 shaking us down & showing us how to trust our roots.

Change is here.

L.O.L

Looking up from my vintage, leathered, strapped journal, I successfully grin knowing I've fluidly completed 3 original poems. *(This one will be the 4th for today.)* A brave robin comes to visit me on my deck. *(I love birds, such fascinating, feathered creatures.)*
I'm so thankful to be in nature and be able to write simultaneously. *(Both among some of my fav things in life.)* I'm so thankful to be this close to a bird that trusts his stance near me. I'm ecstatic to see it take a shit right on top of the ledge of my deck—a nice bright, white splat over the once vibrant, red deck. He just exudes such determined, straightforward confidence. I guess we all need to release a little of what no longer serves us – no matter who's watching!

As I Ground

As I ground
I hear Thunder, my singing bowl.

As I ground
I see Lighting, my arrow.

As I ground I taste Rain, my purifier.

As I ground
I breathe Wind, my voice.

Simple Reminders

Splash in the Water Play with the Earth Whisper to the Sky Dance in your Fire

Keep Peddling

That holiday feeling slowly slips away
like a parent letting go of the bicycle...
hoping their child will pick-up the rhythm on their own.

Cycles

Grounded in Summer &
s t r e t c h i n g toward Winter, the buds in Spring are like
   goosebumps. Shaking off what no longer serves... those
   colors *F a l l* again
and reflect, an abundant life.

That is all

I want the freedom to be more concise.

Flickering

The afternoon has seeped into my room again.
This time, flickering around curiously through my papers.
    Unearthing my meditation spots.
Revealing my overdue goals.
I admire this brave light and revel in its warmth. I find
    comfort here.
I dream bigger here. I ground longer here.

Summer is near.

Can You Use It in a Sentence?

There are some words not used enough anymore. Words that haven't graced most pages, or rolled off enough tongues. Maybe these should be our mantras for the New Year or affirmations for the day. I know which one will be mine. Can you use yours in a sentence?

Remarkable Exquisite Luxuriant Wispy Voluminous Courteous Rippled Extraordinary Revolutionary Mottled Prickly Tenacious Equipped Elated Ecstatic Arduous

Words Neglected, Part 2

Words have texture. Some we can wear, see, drink, hold, throw, hug, love, dislike, teach, create, tear down.

Some are:

Abrasive Blemished Cottony Dehydrated Etched Flaky Grungy Hazy Inflated Jarring Knobbed Lustrous Mosaic Numbing Ornamented Pliable Reflective Scarred Tingly Unctuous Velvety Withered Yielding

Daily Lessons from Trees

Inhale & stretch Exhale & ground Sway the storms
Embrace the bare Bud your own pace Rest in the
Shade Build solid trust Nourish your soul Reveal your
auras Shed & release Sleep to renew

Bouquet

If every flower were a thought,
a person, a place,
a memory, a feeling,
I would have the most compelling arrangement of time &
 space.

Defining Moment

If I was ever interviewed by a journalist, or someone on the red carpet, and they asked me..."*What are your deepest fears?*" My answer might be....

"Oh yeah, I have tons of those! I fear not using my gift to its fullest potential; wasting it on procrastination, laziness or overwhelment. I fear not realigning with my passion for writing. I fear someone else writing my story. But the worst fear of all...is not having anything else to write. You know, the ink drying up. I fear not being able to see my words. Not being able to feel my story. No moods left to convey or decode--that everything that could ever be written, has already been told. I think that's worse than writer's block."

Promise to Sunrise

How ironic I needed saving, as I sat on the cool sand, by
    an abandoned lifeguard chair.

When I look back at this photographic memory, I realize,
    I was saved the moment I arose that day,
before the sun kissed the sea.

I keep this picture hung on my wall to remind myself of
    what thrives my soul.

I keep this picture hung on my wall to remind myself the
    power of saying no, and leaving situations that never
    aligned.

I keep this picture hung on my wall to remind myself of
    why I needed to watch the sunrise that day.

I keep this picture hung on my wall to remind myself
    of my
passions in life, that these are attainable, that I can

survive doing what I love, despite what others fear I can't.

I keep this picture hung on my wall as a reminder *that I did save myself that day*, even though I had no concrete plan away from the mess.

I keep this picture hung on my wall as a promise to sunrise every day.

About the Author

Andrea R. Freeman is the author of *Messages From My Grandparents in Heaven; How You Can Keep Contact With Yours*. Her poem *Extensions* was selected & published in the 2023 Pennsylvania Bards Eastern PA Poetry Book Review. You can find Andrea reading her poetry at the Bethlehem, PA Barnes & Noble Open Mic Nights, where she was also a featured poet there. She is currently working on a card deck for writers, scrapbook art featuring her poetry and leading a journaling workshop. Andrea, her husband Anthony and fur son Bucky, live in Pennsylvania.

instagram.com/soul_to_page

About The Photographer

With a passion for photography and love of cinema and recreating an era, Colleen decided to leave the cosmetology industry, and dive head first into a full-time photography career.

She launched Bunnie & Clyde in late 2016, and chose the name to honor her late beloved rabbit, Babs and combined her second love of film. Together with her husband, Anthony they launched Bunnie & Clyde Photography, specializing in portraiture and natural light. Their aim is to help their clients' true personality shine through naturally.

instagram.com/bunie_n_clyde_photography